CANCER

CANCER

22 June–22 July

PATTY GREENALL & CAT JAVOR

MQP

Published by MQ Publications Limited
12 The Ivories
6–8 Northampton Street
London N1 2HY
Tel: 020 7359 2244
Fax: 020 7359 1616
Email: mail@mqpublications.com
Website: www.mqpublications.com

Copyright © MQ Publications Limited 2004
Text copyright © Patty Greenall & Cat Javor 2004

Illustrations: Gerry Baptist

ISBN: 1-84072-662-8

1 3 5 7 9 0 8 6 4 2

Printed in Italy

WHAT IS ASTROLOGY?

Astrology is the practice of interpreting the positions and movements of celestial bodies with regard to what they can tell us about life on Earth. In particular it is the study of the cycles of the Sun, Moon, and the planets of our solar system, and their journeys through the twelve signs of the zodiac—Aries, Taurus, Gemini, Cancer, Leo, Virgo, Libra, Scorpio, Sagittarius, Capricorn, Aquarius, and Pisces—all of which provide astrologers with a rich diversity of symbolic information and meaning.

Astrology has been labeled a science, an occult magical practice, a religion, and an art, yet it cannot be confined by any one of these descriptions. Perhaps the best way to describe it is as an evolving tradition.

Throughout the world, for as far back as history can inform us, people have been looking up at the skies and attaching stories and meanings to what they see there. Neolithic peoples in Europe built huge stone structures such as Stonehenge in southern England in order to plot the cycles of the Sun and Moon, cycles that were so important to a fledgling agricultural society. There are star-lore traditions in the ancient cultures of India, China, South America, and Africa, and among the indigenous people of Australia. The ancient Egyptians plotted the rising of the star Sirius, which marked the annual flooding of the Nile, and in ancient Babylon, astronomer-priests would perform astral divination in the service of their king and country.

Since its early beginnings, astrology has grown, changed, and diversified into a huge body of knowledge that has been added to by many learned men and women throughout history. It has continued to evolve and become richer and more informative, despite periods when it went out of favor because of religious, scientific, and political beliefs.

Offering us a deeper knowledge of ourselves, a profound insight into what motivates, inspires, and, in some cases, hinders, our ability to be truly our authentic selves, astrology equips us better to make the choices and decisions that confront us daily. It is a wonderful tool, which can be applied to daily life and our understanding of the world around us.

The horoscope—or birth chart—is the primary tool of the astrologer and the position of the Sun, Moon, Mercury, Venus, Mars, Jupiter, Saturn,

Uranus, Neptune, and Pluto at the moment a person was born are all considered when one is drawn up. Each planet has its own domain, affinities, and energetic signature, and the aspects or relationships they form to each other when plotted on the horoscope reveal a fascinating array of information. The birth, or Sun, sign is the sign of the zodiac that the Sun was passing through at the time of birth. The energetic signature of the Sun is concerned with a person's sense of uniqueness and self-esteem. To be a vital and creative individual is a fundamental need, and a person's Sun sign represents how that need most happily manifests in that person. This is one of the most important factors taken into account by astrologers. Each of the twelve Sun signs has a myriad of ways in which it can express its core meaning. The more a person learns about their individual Sun sign, the more they can express their own unique identity.

ZODIAC WHEEL

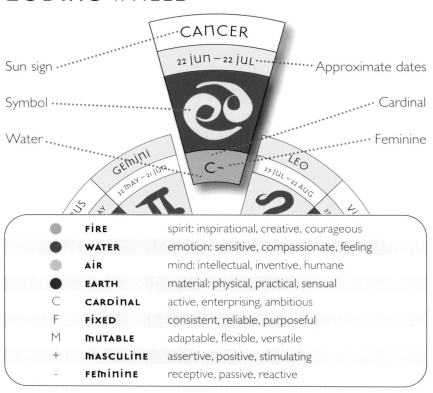

Sun sign · Approximate dates

Symbol · Cardinal

Water · Feminine

CANCER

22 JUN – 22 JUL

C–

GEMINI
22 MAY – 21 JUN

LEO
23 JUL – 22 AUG

●	**FIRE**	spirit: inspirational, creative, courageous
●	**WATER**	emotion: sensitive, compassionate, feeling
●	**AIR**	mind: intellectual, inventive, humane
●	**EARTH**	material: physical, practical, sensual
C	**CARDINAL**	active, enterprising, ambitious
F	**FIXED**	consistent, reliable, purposeful
M	**MUTABLE**	adaptable, flexible, versatile
+	**MASCULINE**	assertive, positive, stimulating
–	**FEMININE**	receptive, passive, reactive

PART ONE

THE ESSENTIAL
CANCER

RULERSHİPS

Cancer is the fourth sign of the zodiac, the first of the Water signs, and it is ruled by the Moon. Its symbol is the Crab. Cancer is a Cardinal and Feminine sign. There are earthly correspondences of everything in life for each of the Sun signs. The parts of the human body that Cancer represents are the stomach and the breast, and it also represents the metal silver. Gemstones for Cancer are pearl, quartz crystal, moonstone, chalcedony, and opal. Cancer also signifies home, family, and tradition, and great rivers, springs, gardens, cellars, bathrooms, and baths, as well as baking and cooking. It is also associated with cabbages, cucumbers, cheese, milk and dairy, melons, mushrooms, pumpkins, squashes, turnips, white roses, lilies, and poppies, and also with mothers and carers.

CANCER

The parts of the human body that Cancer represents are the stomach and the breast.

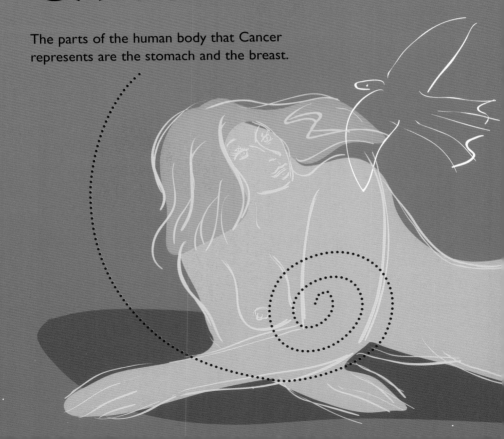

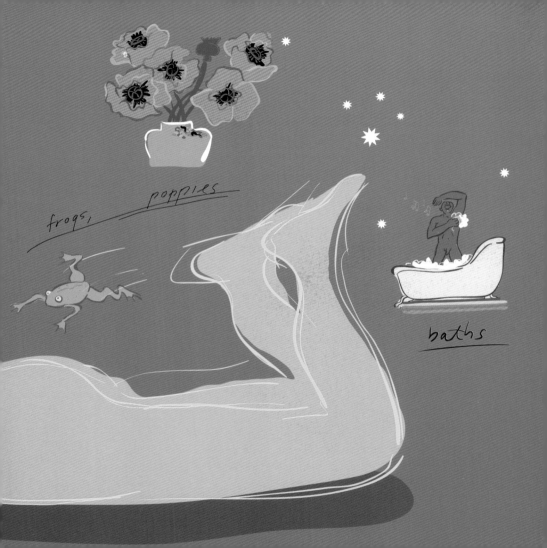

frogs, poppies

baths

PERSO⊙∩ALİTY

Keeping in mind that Cancer is the sign that rules home and family, it is not surprising that those born under this sign love their home along with the comfort that home provides. Quite simply, home is where their heart is, and anyone who has a piece of Cancer's heart will also enjoy Cancer's generosity—including home cooking, big hugs, and lots of emotional support. One of the most well-known characteristics of the Cancer personality is the capacity for caring and sharing. It's true, they love to nurture and protect and because they are such intuitive people, they know exactly how to make the object of their affections—whether it's a lover, a child, or anyone else—feel comfortable and cherished. But it's not just people who get smothered with care and attention. A Cancer personality can take anything—an animal, a garden, a project—and immediately be aware of what's needed to encourage it to fulfill its potential. They are in tune with trends and public feeling, so they know intuitively just how to satisfy the needs and desires of the public at large. Cancer also has amazing business acumen, so much so that more millionaires are born under this sign than under any other. And they also tend to accumulate wealth and valuables, which provide them with a shield against those dreaded feelings of want and need that so often threaten their sense of security.

As a Cardinal sign, that is, one of the signs that herald the start of a season, Cancer possesses great skills of leadership and is able to bring about change and act as a guide to others. However, Cancer isn't easy to read or get to know. Like its symbol the Crab, it never appears to go after its goals or show its feelings directly, but instead is always moving sideways, skirting around the edges of something until it is assured of success. Rejection is terribly painful to Cancer personalities so they will always try to make certain that they don't expose themselves to that possibility. Since their sign is a Water sign, their connection to the fluid world of feelings, emotions, and intuition can make them changeable, some would say moody, but this happens only because they so easily absorb the vibes of those around them, and that's something that they're not always aware of. This super-sensitivity also enables them to detect what is going on beneath the surface of a given situation and they use this ability to protect those who are less able to look after themselves, especially children and the elderly.

Of course, some of them are also great thinkers but their natural way of moving through life is instinctive. They can be timid, perhaps even fearful at times, which is why they have such a strong need to establish a sense of safety and security. Like the Crab—a hard shell on the outside yet soft on the inside—they often appear to be tough and resilient even if they're not. Their protective shell also provides them with the safe, secure home that, metaphorically speaking, they can take with them wherever they go. Cancer is a very maternal sign that offers shelter, nourishment, and preservation to others, but it needs to receive these as well. As long as their needs are fulfilled, they can become the ones who look after the needs of others.

Tradition and a sense of connection to a continuing legacy are also extremely important to Cancer. They like to feel part of something that has deep roots, which is why the Cancerians of a family are often the ones who investigate the family tree and who preserve that history for posterity. The Crab is also known for its ability to use its pincers to grip onto something and never let it go. This can manifest itself in many ways, one of which is the way they hang onto the past, both emotionally and also in the sense of hanging onto relics of the past. This makes Cancer people avid collectors; they can either end up with a pile of clutter or, in some instances, a fortune. They particularly treasure objects that have sentimental value but everything they own ends up imbued with memories of some kind. When it comes to people, they'll always be there for those with whom they've developed a kinship, whether through a blood tie or some other attachment. They'll still be there even when that person no longer wishes to continue the relationship. Cancer will find it near-impossible to let go, which some people find comforting, and others not. It does, however, show the commitment that Cancer is capable of. Nobody who has ever been loved by someone born under this sign will ever be excluded from their company or rejected by them unless they have been incredibly cruel or deliberately hurtful.

Cancer personalities also have a singularly wonderful sense of humor. There is a touch of the comic about them; they find everything from the ironies of life to slapstick incredibly funny, and sharing a laugh with their nearest and dearest is what they regard as pure bliss. They also love company, finding nothing more enjoyable than playing host at a table groaning with food, and surrounded by friends and family eating, drinking, and making merry. They adore seeing people at ease and enjoying themselves, and will go out of their way to make sure that every person's particular preferences and comforts are catered for.

A mysterious and alluring quality shines from them and they are imaginative and creative. They find it as elusive to understand their own ever-shifting emotions as everyone else does, yet they show an uncanny talent for understanding what makes others tick. Of all the treasures that they might care to collect, the most valuable is their tender, kind, and loving heart.

CAREER & MONEY

Ruled by the Moon, which traditionally rules the public at large, Cancer has an excellent ability to intuitively tune into people's wants and needs. They have an instinctive awareness that enables them to know just what others want and don't want. They work successfully in the fields of marketing and management; in fact, they are so passionately interested in these subjects that they will even find studying or teaching them compelling and enormously enjoyable. And it's not just in these fields that they are able to use their insight into people's feelings. Looking after other people is one of their main objectives, which is why they also do well in the caring professions— nursing, social work, and teaching. Nor will they ever forget a name or a face, which helps to make them outstanding business people, too.

As a Water sign, Cancer will feel at home in any career that is connected to water. Whether as captain of a ship at sea or operating the controls of a lock on a river, closeness to the tides and to nature's rhythm will keep Cancer feeling both alive and at ease. Water is one of nature's most prolific elements and being of that element, Cancer makes a very productive worker. They are not only excellent gardeners, but also property and business magnates. From just one seed, they can make an orchard or an empire grow, and they're not afraid to get their hands dirty—certainly not when there's something to be gained from it! They also enjoy building and have a natural feel for comfort and convenience when it comes to their own home and office space.

Cancer personalities have amazingly retentive memories and are good at using their store of knowledge to trace the habits or tendencies of people, the money markets, or simply the cost of living. Many become genealogists or business people, or take up work in museums. A number also become artists since they are highly skilled at reproducing visually all that they have stored in their minds. And since Cancerians also have a need for safety and security, they are good at saving money, not just for rainy days but for any kind of day. In other words, they're great at squirreling away their savings—though this doesn't always mean that they're the ones to turn to when you need a loan. They will always look after their own interests first or else how would they be capable of looking after others?

When it comes to work and career, Cancerians' leadership qualities enable them to inspire others to action, and with their special regard for the past and their inclination toward acquiring knowledge, they make good historians and photographers. Their acquisitiveness and their tendency never to throw anything away "just in case" also mean that many decide to make their living as antique dealers.

THE CANCER **CHILD**

The need for comfort and security that Cancer children feel will be evident from the moment they come into the world; they will be very vocal in their demands to be held close and fed often. This powerful hunger for nurturing plays an enormous part in their changing moods. Most parents might expect that they are free for a few moments to get on with other things when their Cancer child is giggling happily and playing with toys, but a moment later, and for no apparent reason, the child suddenly erupts into floods of tears. However, as soon as they hear a few gentle words and are cuddled and played with, their little face will light up again with joy and laughter.

These are sensitive, gentle, and imaginative children and because a sense of safety and protection is so important to them, they develop a protective and caring nature toward those younger and smaller than themselves. They become very attached to all their toys, particularly the soft, fluffy ones, and will treasure them long after they've grown out of them. Home, of course, is their world and that is where they are confident and playful. New, unfamiliar environments may make them shy, but this only lasts as long as it takes them to figure out if there are any danger zones around, or until they find a friend, and then they will pop out of their shell and be rather outgoing. Cancer children are quick to laugh and just as quick to cry: they take it very personally when friends treat them in an offhand manner.

Adolescent Cancerians will constantly check the emotional "atmosphere" for any threat, while putting on a brave face to protect themselves against the insensitivity of others. This can lead to their developing a cliquey group of friends or remaining in a world of their own and becoming grumpy should anyone try to draw them out. They need to be taught that it isn't always a personal attack when someone doesn't agree with them. On the whole, however, a young Cancer is a loving, caring person with a wonderful sense of humor. It's a joy to have them around.

PERFECT GIFTS

Cancer people will treasure any present that makes their home a more comfortable place—a set of cushions, a throw, a blanket, or a quilt cover are always welcome. Any gift will be accepted as a symbol of friendship and attachment. They value homemade gifts as proof of loved ones' creative skills and the personal touch attached to something made specially for them. Cancerians love memorabilia and nostalgic gifts—a specially chosen antique knickknack, a picture book, some photographs of life in the past, or even a camera to record the history of their own life. A photograph album would really warm their heart, especially one filled with photos of their family.

Another real treat for them would be a warm, cozy jumper to make them feel embraced and protected. Pearls, moonstones, or opals are must-haves for jewelry and silver is the preferred metal. Any piece of jewelry that reminds them of days gone by would be cherished, especially a locket for a photograph of a loved one or a charm bracelet for collecting charms with special associations.

FAVORITE FOODS

Cancerians usually come into their element at mealtimes since food represents a mother's love and gives a sense of security in the bosom of the family. They like to keep to a strict mealtime schedule and rarely skip meals because food for them is often the be-all and end-all. Therefore it shouldn't come as a surprise that comfort foods such as dairy products—yogurt, cheese, ice-cream, and chocolate—are high on the list of all but the lactose-intolerant born under this sign. They are renowned for their sweet tooth, so no meal would be complete without at least two helpings of dessert, which means that unless they are very active, they may have a tendency toward weight gain. But they won't leave any of the essential food groups out of their gastronomic repertoire; they eat fruit, vegetables, meats, fish, and grains all with equal pleasure. When they are out shopping for food, Cancerians will always stock up to excess, just in case an unexpected visitor calls. No guest of theirs will ever leave feeling hungry.

Breakfast will consist of either yogurt with lashings of honey, or a bowl of cereal swimming in milk, and it may also include a cooked breakfast of bacon and eggs with all the trimmings. Lunch could be anything from a gourmet sandwich and piece of fruit, to a sit-down, three-course meal at a local restaurant. In the evening, when other people might feel that, after the day's two substantial meals plus morning and afternoon tea, they only want something light, a Cancer can still manage a large bowl of pasta, a big serving of garlic bread, a salad and a cheeky chocolate mousse.

FASHION & **STYLE**

When it comes to fashion and style sense, Cancer people are unlikely to spend hours poring over magazines for the latest fashion craze. They are rather traditional in their tastes, preferring to emulate the clothing of people they respect and admire rather than go with a fashion trend. They may also be inclined to follow the advice of friends and family members whom they love and trust, and if a particular outfit of theirs has received admiring glances and comments, then they will always keep an eye out for similar styles and colors when they are next shopping. In this way, over time, Cancerians will build up a wardrobe of timeless classics—clothes that never date or go out of fashion, and that, with the addition of fashionable accessories, can always be adapted to reflect current trends.

Casual clothes often take up an enormous amount of drawer space because comfort is of major concern to the Cancer clotheshorse. This means that they won't squeeze themselves into skin-tight jeans just because that's what everyone is wearing, and they will reject scratchy, irritating fabrics in favor of soft, cozy materials that are gentle on their sensitive skin. They'll cut out the label, even on designer clothes, if it rubs them up the wrong way. Cancerians can usually get away with wearing any color or pattern they like; their ruler, the Moon, is reflective by nature, which means that so long as they dress to suit their mood, what they wear will suit them. However, if they are planning on making a big impact, then soft grays and silvery shades of blue, green, and beige will do the trick nicely.

İDEAL HOMES

No matter what decoration Cancerians choose for their homes, what's essential is their creature comforts. Their home is their castle; it's where they need to feel safe, protected, and happy and they like it to be a place where they can totally chill. They also have a shrewd understanding of what makes other people feel good; their home will reflect this sensitivity so it will always be a place where friends and loved ones feel warm and coddled.

If you visit a Cancer home, chances are you'll smell the aroma of freshly baked bread or freshly brewed coffee, or a delicious home-cooked meal. Any visit there will be a total comfort experience, with not only lovely aromas like these wafting through the house, but also with comfy chairs and sofas, cozy throws, and soft plumped-up cushions that simply beg visitors to come and sit down. And don't be surprised to find some mood music playing in the background; Cancerians are sure to set the scene perfectly for complete relaxation. They will also always offer a drink and some homemade food, perhaps a snack or maybe, if you're already one of the clan, a full meal including starter and dessert. The cushioned coziness is enough to make anyone want to stay and never leave—which is exactly what Cancer wants!

PART TWO

RISING SIGNS

WHAT IS A **RISING** SIGN?

Your rising sign is the zodiacal sign that could be seen rising on the eastern horizon at the time and place of your birth. Each sign takes about two and a half hours to rise — approximately one degree every four minutes. Because it is so fast moving, the rising sign represents a very personal part of the horoscope, so even if two people were born on the same day and year as one another, their different rising signs will make them very different people.

It is easier to understand the rising sign when the entire birth chart is seen as a circular map of the heavens. Imagine the rising sign — or ascendant — at the eastern point of the circle. Opposite is where the Sun sets — the descendant. The top of the chart is the part of the sky that is above, where the Sun reaches at midday, and the bottom of the chart is below, where the Sun would be at midnight. These four points divide the circle, or birth chart, into four. Those quadrants are then each divided into three, making a total of twelve, known as houses, each of which represents a certain aspect of life. Your rising sign corresponds to the first house and establishes which sign of the zodiac occupied each of the other eleven houses when you were born.

All of which makes people astrologically different from one another; not all Cancerians are alike! The rising sign generally indicates what a person looks like. For instance, people with Leo, the sign of kings, rising, probably walk with a noble air and find that people often treat them like royalty. Those that have Pisces rising frequently have soft and sensitive looks and they might find that people are forever pouring their hearts out to them.

The rising sign is a very important part of the entire birth chart and should be considered in combination with the Sun sign and all the other planets!

THE **RISING SIGNS** FOR CANCER

To work out your rising sign, you need to know your exact time of birth—if hospital records aren't available, try asking your family and friends. Now turn to the charts on pages 38–43. There are three charts, covering New York, Sydney, and London, all set to Greenwich Mean Time. Choose the correct chart for your place of birth and, if necessary, add or subtract the number of hours difference from GMT (for example, Sydney is approximately ten hours ahead, so you need to subtract ten hours from your time of birth). Then use a ruler to carefully find the point where your GMT time of birth meets your date of birth—this point indicates your rising sign.

CANCER WITH **ARIES** RISING

The individual who has the Sun in Cancer with Aries rising has grown up with a strong family foundation and has a direct and unabashed approach to life. They tend to meet challenges head-on, and often with much success, thanks to the early support and encouragement they got at home. In some ways, they identify themselves with a certain family trait, but they're not always grateful for this or at ease with it. They may rebel and try to go their own way, only to find that those who have gone before them have made a similar journey or have adopted a similar attitude. Whatever their intentions, there will always be some dynastic motivation attached to them. They love to create something that has its roots in the past but will stand the test of time and attain new heights of achievement. Their image and the way others perceive or judge them is very important to them; they crave respect and wish to command authority. They feel a powerful need to belong both in their family and in their milieu but they must also be seen as having control over their own destiny.

CANCER WiTH **TAURUS** RiSiNG

Clever, charming, and graceful, but perhaps not very quick. That's how this Cancer moves in the world, and it's not such a bad thing. They're the ones who work hard and get where they're going slowly and surely until they reach the point where they're comfortably well-off. As lovers of art, nature, and beauty in all its forms, they're fond of any activities that give them a chance to indulge this love. Cancerians with Taurus rising are focused on communication and writing, but often their early experiences of school and learning don't hold great memories for them, perhaps because they were always being compared to others. Bonds with siblings are important and if they don't have brothers and sisters, that can be an issue. On the whole, however, they are very self-reliant and practical, preferring to chart their own course toward a life of comfort and luxury. They have a calm acceptance of all that life throws at them and their gentle, caring, and sympathetic nature makes them extremely attractive to almost everyone they meet. This individual truly flourishes later in life, when they end up being not only good listeners, but also having a tremendous ability to communicate thoughts and ideas.

CANCER WiTH GEMiNi RiSiNG

This is one seriously chatty Cancer! Gemini rising bestows the gift of gab, and that says a lot, since Cancer isn't known for being a big talker. You'd do best to avoid chit-chat with them, especially if you only want to hear about what's going on in their life. Others have recognized that Cancerians truly seem to have their finger on the pulse, but they tend not to talk about their true objectives, which are often related to the accumulation of possessions. You shouldn't gauge their worth according to what they own or how much they have in the bank, for these Cancerians have many more admirable talents and skills. That being said, this quick-thinking individual has a considerable knack for intuiting just what the public wants and is willing to pay for. They make brilliant merchants and can seize an opportunity to turn a profit without even breaking sweat. Their sense of humor is considerable; they enjoy laughing at the absurdities of life more than most people, and will often be found at a dinner table playing the part of the witty raconteur and entertaining everyone with amusing anecdotes.

CANCER WITH **CANCER** RISING

The Cancer with Cancer rising comes into the world at daybreak and, like the Sun coming up over the horizon, seems to radiate light and warmth. With their big, shining smile, they influence others and enliven their surroundings, especially their home, which will be inviting and comfortable. They are demonstrative, tactile, warm, and willing to embrace everyone. The Cancer with Cancer rising is endowed with many gifts and is an optimist with a sunny outlook on life. They're sensitive to every emotional undercurrent, and will do anything they can to calm the ragged feelings of those they love. They're also imbued with a powerful sentimental streak and delight in those moments when they can share sweet memories with others and come over all warm and fuzzy. They have a powerful imagination, which serves them well in any creative career, and they also possess an uncanny intuition. They'll be the soul of discretion should anyone wish to let them in on any secrets, and they'll repay any kindness shown to them tenfold.

CANCER WITH **LEO** RISING

Make room and bow for the Cancer with Leo rising! They have a big presence and although it doesn't seem possible, there's even more to this personality than is apparent on the surface. In fact, in many ways this Cancer is the gentle sort of individual seeking comfort, safety, and security, despite coming across as not having a care in the world. They can be as moody and broody as any Cancer, but they simply don't like to show it. Instead, they reveal their lovely bright side to the world—at least most of the time. The Cancerians with Leo rising are the type to bestow favors and give generously of their time and understanding to any who have been granted access to their inner circle. They show great generosity of spirit and take enormous pride in the successes of their nearest and dearest. However, if they don't feel admired by them in return, a dark cloud will descend over their emotions. They're highly strung and highly intuitive individuals whose imagination and creativity know no bounds. If they have the security that is so important to them, they could achieve anything.

CANCER WITH VIRGO RISING

Being on the shy and timid side, Cancer with Virgo rising enjoys having a support network—people who provide a safe environment. They have a lot to offer in terms of friendship as they're caring, easy to get to know, and concerned about the well-being of those they have formed a bond with. They're also neat and tidy and always seem to be clued up on the latest health and exercise craze. In fact, going to the gym is a regular pastime of theirs, especially if they can meet up there with people they know. Their love of nature means that they're often a pet owner and have the sort of pet that needs exercise and provides companionship on long walks. Everything and everyone is of interest to this Cancer. They draw enormous comfort from being with people, particularly those who display a powerful humanitarian spirit. They're into socializing and clubs that are connected to some hobby or interest. They'll often be the first to put their name down for extracurricular activities in the workplace, such as the book group or the fine-dining club. And yet, there is an individuality about them that is stunningly original. Modest and thoughtful, they're quiet achievers with a shrewd, innovative mind that ensures their considerable success.

CANCER WITH **LIBRA** RISING

It would be hard to ignore the Cancer with Libra rising, who really stands out in a crowd. They are generally good-looking and have the kind of confidence that usually accompanies such looks. They're the ones who can get from the bottom to the top of a company in record time. However, they still have the same need for a safe, secure environment as other Cancerians, it's just that success comes much more easily to them. All they have to do is smile and bat their eyelashes a few times. Having life run smoothly helps motivate them to show a courteous and agreeable face to the world, for they find it hard to tolerate arguments or unpleasant scenes. Their emotional antennae are so finely tuned that any disruption to the harmony they try to create leaves them in a state of depression. However, they're not the type to allow anything to spoil their plans; they'll quickly perk up, go on a charm offensive, and have everyone smiling in no time. Making a good impression is very important to them, and they'll do their best to show and gain respect by always being immaculately turned out, whatever the occasion.

CANCER WITH **SCORPIO** RISING

The Cancer with Scorpio rising knows everything and is the sage of all Cancerians, but they're not boasters. They have a quiet but intense presence and are always switched on, but no one is quite sure what's going on inside their head. Ask them a question and they'll have an answer. They're the fount of all wisdom, and this has nothing to do with how much schooling they've had, although it would be just like them to have a penchant for knowledge and learning. Much of what they know is pure insight; they can see through any prank and anyone who tries to pull the wool over their eyes is doomed to failure. They appear to be incredibly in control, not just of their emotions but of every other aspect of their life. These Crabs are of the armor-plated kind and it will be a rare and special somebody who's allowed to penetrate their shell and reach their soft, sweet inner nature. The need for self-preservation forms part of their relationships with others, though when it comes to leisure pursuits, they love wide open spaces and won't shirk if there's an element of danger.

CANCER WITH **SAGITTARIUS** RISING

Adventure, horseplay, and laughter are only part of what Cancer with Sagittarius rising is made of. They know how to have a good time and can cheer up the most downtrodden soul with their good humor, yet they're also capable of turning off their raucous behavior and tuning into the needs of those around them. They'll know when others have had enough because they possess a natural sensitivity that enables them to know just what people need at any given moment. It doesn't mean that they'll do exactly what others want, for they're staunch individuals with a mind of their own. They have a powerful effect on others because they emanate sympathy; people sense that they feel things intensely. For all their sociability and enjoyment of fooling around, the Cancerians with Sagittarius rising appear to dance to a different tune. Their view of the world is both broad and deep and their intuitive interpretation of all that they see is uncannily perceptive. They have a progressive mind-set, which stands them in good stead when it comes to seeing opportunities to further their career. They'll go beyond the point where others might think there is nothing more to be gained.

CANCER WITH **CAPRICORN** RISING

Getting a smile out of this individual may not be easy but when they do decide to flash their shiny whites at someone, it will be genuine. They can make others laugh with their wicked, satirical sense of humor, and their straight face just makes their little anecdotes even funnier. They're naturally very interested in people and can see the funny side of life, but they're also cautious, so earning their trust is a real honor. These are earnest individuals with firm ambitions and objectives. They have an idealistic side, which motivates them to do something special with their life; they've come into the world with a mission, and they'll achieve their aims one step at a time. They instinctively know that two heads are better than one and once they form an alliance, they'll stick with it for life. People need them for their sensitivity, stability, and intuitive understanding, and they need others just as much. They might not be the most outwardly demonstrative individuals and may not be happy revealing the depth of their feelings, but they have a powerful craving for affection. However, they'll keep their own affection rigidly in reserve for those whose friendship has stood the test of time.

CANCER WITH AQUARIUS RISING

This person isn't your average, everyday Cancer. In fact, guessing their sign would be a challenge because, although they possess the innate Cancer sensitivity, they may seem very different. They can appear a little quirky and much more gregarious than they really are. Possessing Cancer's strong sense of family, they like the idea of being part of a group, but somehow they don't truly meld. They're not at all clingy, and can even seem aloof, managing to retain their individuality, which is an admirable trait. They can be very effective in the world, particularly when they use their protective instincts on behalf of the brotherhood of man. Their concern for others is sincere; they make the perfect champion of the underdog, and will fight injustice wherever they find it. With Aquarius rising, Cancer combines intuition with inspiration, then adds a dash of imagination. The result is an original, inventive person who is tuned in emotionally and mentally. They're industrious and patient, yet also happy-go-lucky—a real treat!

CANCER WiTH **PiSCES** RiSiNG

⟓ The Cancer with Pisces rising is perhaps the most creative of the different types of Sun sign Cancer. They love children and are inspired by their innocence, unpredictability, and spontaneity. In addition, these Cancerians have a knack for teaching and get totally involved in it, whatever the age of their pupils. They may come across as modest, shy, and retiring when they're in a new and unfamiliar environment, but once they find their comfort zone they'll be highly amusing and will show their lovely sense of humor. They have a great attitude toward fun and partying, but in a quieter way than most Cancer Sun sign people. They may be seen dancing, singing, painting, or knitting; their artistic streak will show itself in a myriad of ways. The Cancer with Pisces rising is drawn toward the mysterious and the unusual. They are incredibly romantic and may surround themselves with images of magical, mythical beings. Their imagination delights in books and stories of the unexpected and fantastical. Their view of life is incredibly individual, yet people may never realize how truly unique they are since they are difficult to pin down. They tend not to follow the crowd but only their own inner, inspirational light.

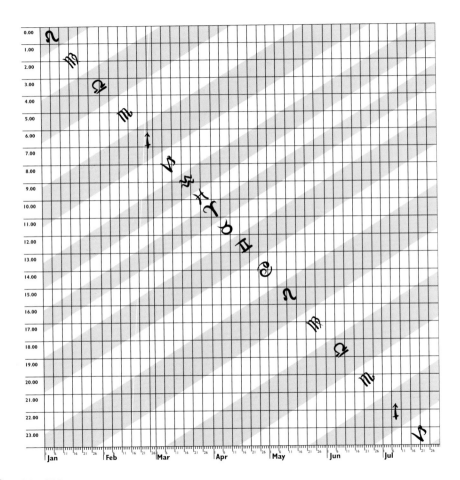

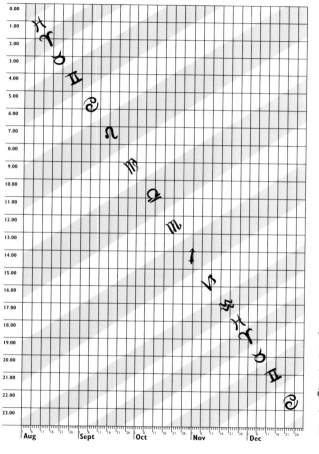

RISING SIGN
CHART

New York
latitude 39N00
meridian 75W00

♈ aries	♎ libra
♉ taurus	♏ scorpio
♊ gemini	♐ sagittarius
♋ cancer	♑ capricorn
♌ leo	♒ aquarius
♍ virgo	♓ pisces

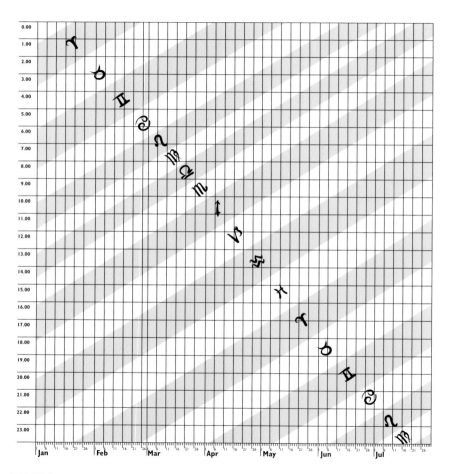

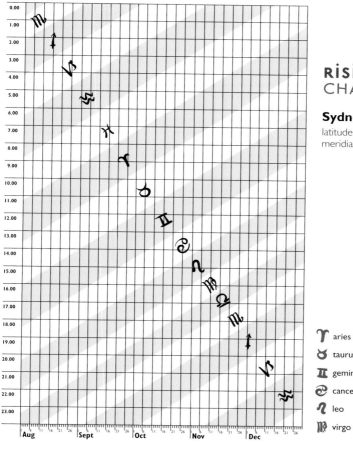

RISING SIGN
CHART

Sydney

latitude 34S00
meridian 150E00

♈ aries		♎ libra	
♉ taurus		♏ scorpio	
♊ gemini		♐ sagittarius	
♋ cancer		♑ capricorn	
♌ leo		♒ aquarius	
♍ virgo		♓ pisces	

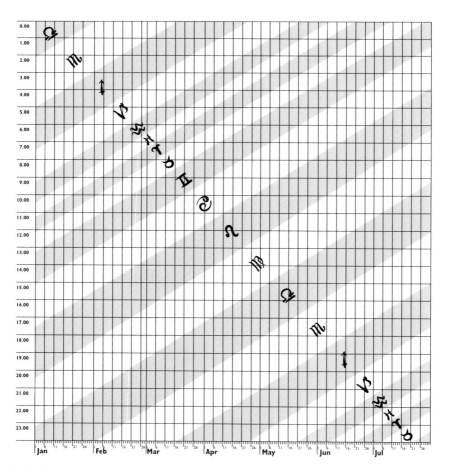

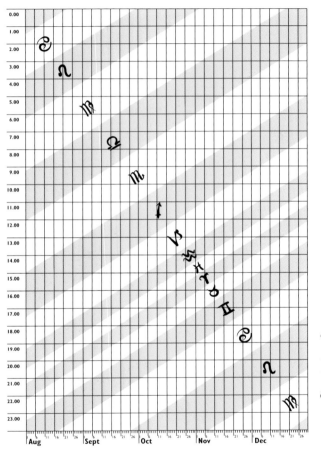

RISING SIGN
CHART

London
latitude 51N30
meridian 0W00

♈ aries	♎ libra
♉ taurus	♏ scorpio
♊ gemini	♐ sagittarius
♋ cancer	♑ capricorn
♌ leo	♒ aquarius
♍ virgo	♓ pisces

PART THREE

RELATIONSHIPS

THE **CANCER** FRIEND

The gentle, caring, and intuitive nature of Cancerians makes them a close and comforting friend. They may have a number of acquaintances but when they call someone "friend," it means they've made that person part of their extended family. Cancerians will keep people at a polite distance and will hold out for a long time before allowing anyone to penetrate their shell. They'll scuttle back and forth and sideways like a Crab until they can get to grips with what the new friend is really like, and provided they feel that the person doesn't threaten or hurt them in any way, Cancerians will hold on tightly, making the new friend feel trusted and secure. Cancer is not looking for fair-weather friends. They are very protective toward the people they become attached to and are brilliant at offering tea and sympathy when they're called for. They have a special gift for understanding the emotional undercurrents in their friends' lives and willingly offer their instinctive insights.

But cozy one-to-one chats on a comfy sofa aren't all that Cancer friends provide; they have a wonderful sense of humor and a wry, comic touch that make them fabulous playmates when they're out on the town. They may, at times, get possessive toward their friends, or clam up and become a little moody when they feel unappreciated or misunderstood, but on the whole, they have an irresistibly sweet, soft center and people love to be near them.

CANCER WITH **ARIES**

Both Aries and Cancer are Cardinal signs, which means that both are dependable and very able, especially in situations where someone needs to take charge. Together they can conquer the world — as long as they can agree ahead of time on who is going to do what. There will be moments when the sensitive Cancer will feel hurt and dismay at being on the receiving end of the tactless hot-tempered Aries tongue, just as Aries will lose patience with having to constantly watch what is said around the Cancer who is prone to tearful, emotional outbursts. But when the chips are down, neither could want for a better champion than the other.

CANCER WITH **TAURUS**

Taurus is honest and won't mess with this sensitive Cancer friend and Cancer intuitively knows how to support the needs of Taurus and will effortlessly offer understanding. There are some similarities between them so they may feel a certain familiarity with one another. Both are sensitive, emotional, and caring, yet they both know how to have a great time. In many ways they are a reflection of one another so they feel a natural rapport. However, Cancer can, on occasion, be changeable, unpredictable, and grumpy, which could destabilize the Bull, who demands constancy and an emotionally safe environment.

CANCER WITH GEMINI

These two make a wonderful comedy double act. They both understand and appreciate the absurdities of life and when they get together, it's as if they are sharing a private joke that the rest of the world just doesn't get. Cancer has a tendency to get a little emotional at times and this may put Gemini in the uncomfortable position of being at a loss for words, just as Gemini may disappoint the Cancer who is in need of sensitivity and sympathy. However, on the whole, they get along well together; the highly intuitive, emotional intelligence of Cancer is offset perfectly by the clever, inventive Gemini mind with its capacity for quick, clear thinking.

CANCER WITH CANCER

Two individuals with the Sun in Cancer could make great friends, so long as they are in sync with one another. When they are good together, they are very, very good. They'll understand each other's wants and needs, and ups and downs, and will be able to support one another through the ebb and flow of this good friendship. But if they're having an off day, then it's another story altogether. Each needs to be in the limelight and if they're fighting over who it's to be, each knows just where to pinch the other so it hurts. With two such hard shells knocking against one another, cracks could develop, so perhaps on days like that it would be best to stay apart.

CANCER WITH **LEO**

Leo is one of the most strong-willed signs of the zodiac—and Cancerians like to have their way, too. As friends, they'll instinctively recognize the other's need for respect and one will usually yield to the other but both will keep a mental tally of who gave in last. They don't regard this as a competition, though. Instead they feel enough affection to want to let the other have their way. When they're in the mood for fun and head out on the town together, no two friends can light up a room quite like these two.

CANCER WITH **VIRGO**

Cancer and Virgo both have an innate gentleness about them, so as friends they get on very well together and will often choose similar things to do. Virgo seems able to contain the sometimes strong emotions of Cancer, while Cancer will encourage Virgo to take more initiative. This friendship will continue to grow because while they both have a different perspective on life, their sense of humor dovetails and they'll find that they enjoy many private jokes together. As a result, they'll feel as if they belong to some kind of exclusive club whose members enjoy plenty of wry amusement and raucous laughter.

CANCER WITH **LIBRA**

Although they won't disagree much, Cancer and Libra have essentially different natures. Libra likes to go to new places, meet new people, party the night away, and enjoy some flirty fun, while Cancerians prefer to party at their old, regular haunts with their familiar circle of pals. Both are very persuasive and like to have their own way, but neither is deliberately stubborn. They could make great friends, but it will just take a while for them to learn to adapt to each other's preferences. But there's enough mutual intrigue for them to combine their interests and build on for the longer term. Perhaps they'll start the party somewhere new then bring it home.

CANCER WITH **SCORPIO**

Cancer and Scorpio friends make a pretty perceptive duo. With just the two of them together, they could probably spend all day discussing what lies behind so and so's antics—and they'd probably have it spot on. There's so much of interest to find out. Both are into talking about people's feelings and motivations and if their gossip sessions turn a trifle bitchy, well, nobody else is listening so nobody ever gets hurt—and at least it provides them with a few giggles. When these two are out with a group of people, they share an unspoken feeling of support and understanding.

CANCER WITH **SAGITTARIUS**

Cancer loves to hear stories of faraway places and far-fetched possibilities and could listen to a glittering Sagittarius tale of adventure the entire day. Quite simply, they are fascinated by the Archer's seemingly inspired life story. But the Archer won't be so impressed by Cancer, except by the fact that Cancer admires them! Sagittarius is prone to flattery but Cancer is actually genuinely interested in Sagittarius, so much so that they could almost be persuaded to leave home for a short time in an attempt to have some similar adventures. This friendship isn't about regular contact; it's more about enjoyable accidental encounters.

CANCER WITH **CAPRICORN**

Not all opposites get on as well together as Cancer and Capricorn. They are both ambitiously minded yet different enough not to actually clash in their aims. As friends, they can always rely on one another and their friendship could last a lifetime. Even when they live thousands of miles apart, they'll still stay in touch. A lot of the attraction is based on a shared sense of life's ironies, which afford them endless opportunities for wry amusement. They find it comforting to be with someone who totally understands how funny the paradoxes of life can be. This is a friendship that gets stronger the more one-on-one encounters they have.

CANCER WiTH **AQUARiUS**

When they look at each other, Cancer and Aquarius see someone very different from themselves. Aquarius loves finding out about what makes people tick, but will probably never understand the depth of emotion in Cancer. Aquarians will either stick with the friendship and try, in vain, to know Cancer better, or will meet up only occasionally because their inability to really understand Cancer will frustrate them. Cancer, on the other hand, will see where Aquarius is coming from and will really admire their humanitarian qualities, but when Aquarius is in the mood for some mental gymnastics, Cancer will simply float away.

CANCER WiTH **PiSCES**

Cancer makes a great buddy for Pisces. Not many people can understand the mysterious nature of Pisces, least of all Pisceans themselves, but Cancer comes very close. Both being a "feelings" type of person, they'll easily tune into one another. But if Cancer gets too moody, Pisces might just do a vanishing act, and if Pisces gets a little too unreliable, good old reliable Cancer will be furious. On the whole, though, these two will enjoy being in each other's company and will always find reasons to spend more time together.

THE CANCER WOMAN IN LOVE

Like everything else in the Cancer woman's life, love is connected to her need for comfort and security; she'll make her choice of partner based on whether she can sense the presence of that strong, emotional bond, which she needs to hold her in a soft and fluffy but, ultimately, safe place. The single Cancer girl looking for love is a strange and subtle creature, who never moves directly or brazenly toward the object of her interest. For example, when she's at a party, you'll see her criss-crossing the room, animatedly joining in this conversation or that group of revelers, while always remaining in sight of the person she wants to get closer to. This eventually affords her the opportunity to join his group and engage him in conversation without ever laying herself open to rejection and hurt. She may even go further with her evasive techniques, forcing him into a friendly argument and pretending that she doesn't agree with him while always keeping a sweet smile on her face so he can't be sure whether she's teasing him or not. In this way, she'll have maneuvered him into a position where all his attention is focused on her, and because she has an abundance of alluring, feminine charm, she'll hold his attention until the end of the evening. But simply because she's spent most of the party getting to know him, it doesn't naturally follow that she'll want to continue with the association once the party's over. Just as she takes her time in getting his attention, so she'll want to make sure that he can hold hers as well.

The Cancer woman is looking for a relationship in which she can comfortably move from one aspect of her nature to the other. On the one hand she's the protective mother, who will cook and cater for her man and provide the springboard from which he can go out into the world and achieve all the greatness and financial success she expects from him. On the other, she's the playful child who wants fun and laughter and who wants to be indulged, cosseted, and cherished. She'll give of herself generously to the man with whom she has a deep, emotional connection, as long as he makes the effort to love and protect her, but she won't allow her gentle heart to be taken advantage of.

Once she's made a commitment, the Cancer woman sets about creating a safe and secure place for their love to grow; she's expert at knowing what makes the perfect domestic bolt hole—the place where they can both find comfort and solace. She'll make sure that they're surrounded by treasures and souvenirs of their time together, to act as constant reminders of their joint history. The memories they amass will help in forging an ever stronger familial bond. The Cancer woman is possessive, not just of the mementos of their past, but of him, too, and she won't find it easy to let go of the relationship even after it is long past its sell-by date. She will cling on to the bitter end and her heart will hold steady, just like a Crab's claw. Then, just as a Crab sheds its shell and grows a new one, her heart will renew itself and she'll feel the same powerful emotions, depth of feeling, and loving tenderness when a new love comes along.

CANCER WOMAN WITH ARIES MAN

In love: The Aries man arrives on the scene like a knight in shining armor and the Cancer woman is the maiden he intends to rescue. She'll think he's wonderful and there's absolutely no doubt he'll be attracted to her and will proceed to try to make everything right in her life. When the Cancer woman uses her feminine wiles and looks devotedly into the eyes of her Aries man, the flattery he feels is enough to undo him. But this man doesn't know the meaning of patience. He can't handle situations that are dripping with emotion, whereas the Cancer girl thrives on emotional energy and is very romantically inclined. Although her heart is susceptible to his heroic nature, she needs to know her man has a deep capacity for real love and powerful emotions. The Aries man does have that capacity, but he doesn't express it in a way she can always recognize. He'll love her as long as she's happy but unfortunately, he has very little patience when dealing with emotional outbursts. He will try, but however hard he tries, his efforts are unlikely to meet her standards. He's happy to go along with her other quirks — like the regular visits she makes to her family — and he might even enjoy them. She'll honestly believe she's good for him because she'll encourage him to nurture family ties. This is a love that will grow but will need assistance from friends and family.

In bed: When the Cancer woman is in the mood for sex, she'll find the Aries man definitely worth stripping down for, at least once. If she's ever emotionally overwrought and floundering in a sea of tears, he'll probably not even notice. This can actually be very helpful because she'll quickly forget her troubles once her mind and heart are focused on his hot-blooded embrace. She should think of him as a sex therapist — someone who is so passionately expressive and sexually demanding that while her body is entwined in his she'll be able to think of nothing else. He'll make her forget her tears, and possibly even the reason for them. He's fascinated by the way her changing mood can make her appear to be a different woman, yet somehow the same one he fell for. He'll be delighted at the possibility of being able to show off his bedroom prowess to an endless array of delectable females. Her multi-faceted nature will keep the Aries man happy, so she can rest assured that he won't stray. He knows how to handle her in bed, that's for sure! He's a horny devil who's ripe and ready at the slightest innuendo and he'll see the possibilities in the most mundane acts.

CANCER WOMAN WITH **TAURUS MAN**

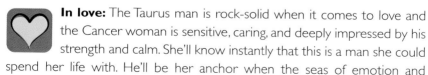 **In love:** The Taurus man is rock-solid when it comes to love and the Cancer woman is sensitive, caring, and deeply impressed by his strength and calm. She'll know instantly that this is a man she could spend her life with. He'll be her anchor when the seas of emotion and

insecurity get a bit rough and, like her Atlas, will keep her supported. Added to that, he's honest and won't play around with her, which fulfills perfectly her need for safety and security. The Cancer woman's ability to cater intuitively to his every need is very attractive to the Taurus man, who wants his woman to be a truly feminine provider of comfort, food, and affection. He wants to spend time cuddled up on a sofa with her, with tasty food and fine wine on the coffee table in front of them. This scene looks extremely seductive to the Cancer woman, because the safer and more secure she feels, the more she gives of her sweet and gentle heart. As he is so good at providing the luxurious, expensive, and romantic indulgences that make her feel special and loved, this is a mutually heart-warming relationship. Both are highly sentimental creatures, so anniversaries are unlikely to be forgotten. In fact, close friends and family will try to stay away because the cute intimacy and private exchanges between these two can get embarrassing for others. But this closeness is, indeed, the glue that binds them together.

In bed: The Taurus man unleashed is not a force to underestimate. There's nothing delicate about the way he expresses his sexual urges. He'll grunt and groan like a bull but, aside from that, the Taurus man is an excellent lover. Lady Cancer will be a little bemused at first, but this uninhibited behavior is just what she's always dreamed of in a man. His unrestrained sexual manner allows her to abandon everything—fears, clothes, and anything else that could possibly stand in the way of total intimacy. The Taurus man will wrap his lunar lady up in his powerful embrace and press his body firmly against hers. Yes, he's very, very physical. She'll melt into his arms and feel so wanted and needed that she will be able to throw off any and all insecurities. She could even surprise herself with her new-found wanton sexiness. Nothing will stop her now. The Taurus man will have found his match and will be reveling in what he perceives as a stroke of luck. On occasion, he'll be clumsy and even a bit crude in his pillow talk. This would normally be a turn-off to the sensitive Cancer girl, but his gentle touch is comforting and he's so practiced at giving pleasure, that she may even find it funny. At any rate, a little giggling will only heighten her arousal— and his—but no teasing, please, he's in earnest.

CANCER WOMAN WiTH GEMiNi MAN

In love: The Gemini man has the ability to set off the Cancer woman's intrigue radar simply by walking into the room. She finds him attractive and lovable, and intuitively knows what makes him tick. It amuses her to see his childlike enthusiasm in action, and the stories he tells make her imagination work overtime. Her beguiling femininity simply spurs him on to try to capture her attention even more. He'll make her laugh—and cry. He's a marathon talker, so she'll always know what he's thinking, but he doesn't speak about his feelings as much as she'd like. Although she has a certain amount of intuition, she can only be aware of what he's feeling some of the time. She could teach him a thing or two about expressing his feelings, but he may tire of hearing what she has to say on the subject because it gets a little too close to the bone for his liking. He doesn't know how to handle such matters unless he takes things very slowly, one step at a time. Meanwhile the Gemini man may be able to teach her about less intense human relationships. He's got lots of friends and knows how to surf on the crest of life, but he may only ever skim the surface of her emotions, setting off ripples that excite her but never move her deep down. If it feels good, they should go for it, but they'll need to learn to express their feelings in a way that both can understand.

 In bed: The Gemini man is into tickling and teasing with fingertips and feathers. Even when the Cancer lady takes the initiative—which she'll do frequently—he seems to be in charge and is never short of a new game to play or a different place to try out a new technique, whether on her body or in some new location. He'll drive his Cancer lover mad with so much pleasurable foreplay that, as he takes her to the brink over and over again, she might even discover a demanding, impatient, and pleading side to her sexual persona. He's got a wicked sense of fun and she'll enjoy lying back and watching with amusement as he scampers all over her body, drawing responses from erogenous zones that she didn't even know she had until she met him. She wants to be able to pleasure him as much as he does her, but his dexterous skill and playful imagination seem to fill all the gaps. It really excites him to see the effect he can have on this enchanting woman. Next to his boundless energy and enthusiasm, she may begin to feel inadequate, though needlessly so. She has to learn simply to accept his gift of pleasure; after all, he thoroughly enjoys offering it. But for all his clever skills, the amusing fun and games only touch her superficially. This Cancer lady could soon feel frustrated in her desire for a more intense and profound emotional relationship.

CANCER WOMAN WITH **CANCER MAN**

In love: When the Cancer woman first meets him, the Cancer man may seem like any other guy but gradually, as they learn to trust one another and begin to show their vulnerabilities, they'll find a mutual sense of solace and an ability to lovingly contain one another. They will definitely make a home together, otherwise what would be the point of the relationship? Both need to make a place to call their own, and as quickly as possible. Their relationship will grow and grow, and having shared interests alongside their shared cares and concerns will give this love a very secure foundation. In fact, the more time they spend doing things together and taking photographs to remind them of their life together, the stronger the ties that bind will grow. But since both of them are so sensitive and empathic, this partnership could be a bit of an emotional roller-coaster; one of them could be up when the other's down unless they synchronize their inner rhythms. The home they make together will be filled with laughter and tears—both of which, when it comes to two people born under the sign of Cancer, provide them with a bonding experience. In the case of these two, the couple that cries together, stays together. With such a pairing it would be unusual if the subject of children weren't raised early on in their relationship. That way, each will know where the other stands on the subject, and chances are that they'll agree. Both want little ones to look after; it's in their stars!

 In bed: The Cancer man's embracing style is not for everyone but it will certainly make his Cancer lady feel safe enough to let go of any inhibitions. She'll be thrilled at having found a lover to whom she can show her soft underbelly, and know that he'll handle her sensitivity with all due care and attention. Feelings are what it's all about with these two Crabs and they're perfectly in tune with one another on that score, despite all the toing and froing and sideways scuttling that takes place before they actually get down to things. But it's a fated attraction; they just know that they're right for each other from the moment they first lay eyes on one another. That's when each will make the decision to go for it. Both of them are highly sensitive to touch, and the responses that they can draw from each other are immediate and very sexy. Hugging, snuggling, and making love is a deeply emotional experience, which bonds them more closely each time they're together. When these two Crab lovers are gripping one another and holding on through the throes of fierce passion, wild elephants couldn't drag them apart. But to anyone watching their seduction routine, how they actually got into this clinch would be a mystery. Both of them are very subtle in the way they give off sexual signals; they shuffle around the edges, always moving sideways, until they're sure the other is as interested as they are. And then they pounce!

CANCER WOMAN WITH LEO MAN

 In love: If he's the king of the zodiac, then she's the queen. They are like joint monarchs; eternally loyal and loving, and with a powerful need to procreate. And since they are also the Sun and Moon, they never get too immersed in the dark side of life, moving through it as if in an eternal dance. The love between these two has the potential to maintain a shining and dignified balance. Theirs is a partnership that offers mutual respect and regard, with each of them aware that they can complement the other beautifully. However, being aware of something doesn't mean that they'll do it. At the end of the day, it all comes down to the simple mix of the elements—Fire and Water. When fiery Leo man pompously lays down the law, he has the ability to make his watery Cancer girl boiling mad, and if he doesn't back off and give her the chance to cool down, then she'll just evaporate right out of this arms. She, on the other hand, could become so clinging and smothering that he'll feel as though he's wrapped in a wet blanket and all his fire will go out, never to return! These two will instinctively know that they are right for each other and if they can both make adjustments so that they meet in the middle, this could be one magnificent match. There will always be arguing, but the Leo man has a big generous heart toward the people he loves and the Cancer lady has a kind heart toward the people she protects and nurtures.

In bed: The Leo man wants to be entertained and the Cancer woman wants to be cherished, so, here's a suggestion. Since Cancer rules the breast and stomach, she should wrap a string of bells around her midriff and do a belly dance for him. He'll love her fun-filled performance and will be more than grateful in return. And she need not worry that she's the only one performing; the Leo man has a penchant for drama and will turn their bedroom experience into a razzmatazz production once he gets into the swing of role-playing. One night he'll be the Rhett Butler of romance and the next, he'll be Tarzan and make his Cancer lady feel like Jane! There's a powerful erotic pull between these two and he can be as generous with his sexual love as he is with gifts. She has a deep capacity to be receptive to the physical love he offers, while he could quite happily drown in her sensual tenderness. On occasion, when he's a bit rough and ready, she may have to put on her hard, outer shell, but as long as he doesn't take her apparent passivity and subtlety to mean that she lacks passion, then these two will get on very nicely in the bedroom.

CANCER WOMAN WITH VIRGO MAN

In love: There's an easy, peaceful feeling about the love between a Cancer woman and a Virgo man. They're not likely to ever let each other down. In fact, they very quickly get into a harmonious rhythm that flows sweetly through the relationship so, "if music be the food of love, play on." It will be a playful relationship, with both of them sharing a sense of friendly amusement about the oddities of life and enjoying the endearing idiosyncrasies of the other. They are very indulgent of each other's foibles and often find that some gentle teasing makes for a lighthearted bonding experience. Both are liable to get a little crabby at times, but if ever there was someone who could make them laugh, then that someone is the other. This is one of those beautifully symbiotic relationships in which each fits the other's vibe perfectly. Although she can be prone to grumpiness and he can be critical, when they are together, their need to sulk or pick will melt away. They're good for each other and their love keeps their hearts happy and healthy. The laughter and companionship they share have a powerful healing effect on them both and the mutual support they gain from the relationship gives each of them the courage to go beyond their normal bounds of personal achievement and revolutionize and revitalize their lives.

In bed: She could get moody, which could cause him to chill or make him start picking on her for being so changeable. He could get critical, which would cause her to retreat into her shell and stay there until he apologizes. But they know each other well, so this behavior could actually be part of their routine, and because there is so much love between them, neither can take any of it too seriously. Funnily enough, these very frustrations are the appetizer to their feast. Despite appearances, a little bit of tension is just what the Cancer woman and Virgo man need to increase their desire to get into each other's arms. They actually enjoy a minor disagreement because of the making-up bit that always comes along afterward. The result of all this is a desperate hunger for each other. The sex is satisfying and comforting—a staple part of their relationship. The Cancer woman has enough flowing sensuality to reach into the depths of her Virgo man's passion, and he'll go weak at the knees and blissfully fall apart as she gently coaxes him to become one with her. The more he holds her and enjoys her sweet caresses, the more he is able to feed her desire and heighten his own. With such mutually responsive passion, it's hard for them to tell where one begins and the other finishes.

CANCER WOMAN WITH LIBRA MAN

 In love: When Libra man is in love, he's more charming and romantic than any prince in a fairytale. He's a gentleman in all possible respects and even if he's one of those rare gentlemen who are a little rough around the edges, he's never crude or uncouth. But despite all his romantic, captivating charm, the Cancer woman may not fall for him immediately because she's naturally cautious and, being rather enchanting herself, knows just how irresistible a touch of fairy glamour can be. But should he ever make up his mind to pursue her, he'll woo her until she simply can't say "no." He'll treat her like a lady, opening doors for her and kissing her hand, and unless she's a militant feminist, she'll turn on her own beguiling charms, which will have a very powerful effect on him indeed. The one hurdle that he'll eventually have to jump with her concerns his fickleness and flirtatiousness. She needs to know that he'll be there for her, and being such an intuitive lady, she'll know whether or not he's serious. Meanwhile he, having been born under an Air sign, likes to be free as a bird, so her clingy tendencies could bring him down. On the whole, however, he's very attracted to the caring, comforting, and nurturing femininity of her character, and her shifting emotions add a touch of mystery that heightens the appeal. They will pursue one another with equal enthusiasm and, given time, could really grow to need the beautiful love that is played out between them.

In bed: Libra is the only sign of the zodiac that is represented by something mechanical and, as it's ruled by the amorous planet Venus, it's sweet all through. As a result, the Libra man is hard to resist; he's nothing less than one smooth-talking, heart-stopping love machine. He knows perfectly well how to make the Cancer woman go weak at the knees. However, the most powerful ingredient in this sexual union is love. If they are to find happiness in each other's arms, love is absolutely essential to both of them. A randy romp around the bedroom might be fun but, ultimately, they'll both end up feeling empty and even a bit lonely. There is potential for variety here, however; a few randy romps alternating with some romantic candlelit trysts will keep them both turned on. The Libra man's need for beauty, harmony, immaculately clean sheets, and fantasy to whet his sexual appetite are things she can be sensitive to, but these won't always give her the feelings of closeness and affection that are so important to her. But where there's a will, there's a way, and once they've caught the other's sexual drift, they'll always be willing to go all the way.

CANCER WOMAN WITH SCORPIO MAN

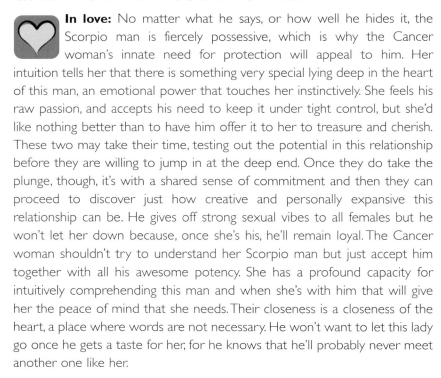 **In love:** No matter what he says, or how well he hides it, the Scorpio man is fiercely possessive, which is why the Cancer woman's innate need for protection will appeal to him. Her intuition tells her that there is something very special lying deep in the heart of this man, an emotional power that touches her instinctively. She feels his raw passion, and accepts his need to keep it under tight control, but she'd like nothing better than to have him offer it to her to treasure and cherish. These two may take their time, testing out the potential in this relationship before they are willing to jump in at the deep end. Once they do take the plunge, though, it's with a shared sense of commitment and then they can proceed to discover just how creative and personally expansive this relationship can be. He gives off strong sexual vibes to all females but he won't let her down because, once she's his, he'll remain loyal. The Cancer woman shouldn't try to understand her Scorpio man but just accept him together with all his awesome potency. She has a profound capacity for intuitively comprehending this man and when she's with him that will give her the peace of mind that she needs. Their closeness is a closeness of the heart, a place where words are not necessary. He won't want to let this lady go once he gets a taste for her, for he knows that he'll probably never meet another one like her.

In bed: Cancer and Scorpio, two Water signs, will have a whale of a time in bed! These two lovers so enjoy being together that even if someone threw them a life preserver, they wouldn't come up to grab it. Who needs air when they can keep on swallowing each other's hot and horny breath! The Scorpio man is so sexually intuitive that even if the Cancer woman put a blindfold on him for an added thrill, he would easily find her pleasure zones. Yes, this couple will most certainly get it on. She may not be able to surprise him, but he'll always be up for her. Any attempt to seduce him may look bungled; instead, all she really has to do is keep up her little sideways dance and be ready with open arms, eyes, and attitude! When these two get into bed together, a tidal wave of passion washes over them and sends them spinning in ecstasy. There's definitely a dangerous quality to his eroticism, which may make her wary but the Scorpio man knows how to coax the Cancer lady out of her shell.

CANCER WOMAN WITH **SAGITTARIUS MAN**

In love: So, the Cancer woman has been out for a night on the town and has met a Sagittarius man. She finds him fascinating and he's definitely interested. He offers to drive her back to her place and she invites him in for a nightcap. She sits next to him on the sofa with her family photo album and he looks at his watch. If she thinks that he'll love her family as much as he loves her, she should think again. Finding common ground for love to grow between a male Archer and a Lady Crab may be like looking for an acre of land between the salt water and the sea shore. These may not be the easiest of people to put together, so no one should try. They are both independently minded, but in different ways, yet if they decide to set their hearts on each other, they could end up doing a romantic tango—forever coming together and moving apart, yet never actually being able to let each other go. There can be something very special between these two, but what it is will be a mystery to everyone else. If they manage to get involved in some activity that they both enjoy—horse riding is one possibility—then there's a chance that they'll spend enough time in each other's company to fall in love. It's best to let them sort it out between them; others should never try to get involved.

 In bed: This is another relationship that combines the elements of Fire and Water. Sometimes the result is a huge explosion of sexual chemistry but at other times it's just a pile of wet soot. If they don't annoy each other they'll have a ton of boiling hot steam between them. Theirs will be an unforgettable experience even if they'd both prefer to put it out of their minds. It's also unrepeatable, which could be good or bad, depending on the peculiarities of the particular Sagittarius man and Cancer woman. Many couples born under these signs—those with a seriously good sense of humor—will have a healthy, happy, and fulfilling sex life together. They'll have a rip-roaring time with plenty of romping and stomping. In fact, this liaison can be downright tempestuous, as they burn up many calories in pursuit of each other. But it will also have an element of danger, which they'll either love or hate. Most Cancer women are too sensitive and clingy for the free-spirited and often tactless Sagittarius man. If she withdraws into her protective shell, he'll think that's the signal for him to go off adventuring in new territory.

CANCER WOMAN WITH **CAPRICORN MAN**

In love: The Cancer woman and the Capricorn man could easily grow old together, though they may do it before they reach 30! These are opposite signs of the zodiac, so they'll attract one another like magnets then settle in for the long haul. When they are together, they are one, like the yin-yang symbol—opposites that together create the prerfect union. There's a degree of comfort and mutual approval between them that makes this link very close, and everything seems so natural between them. Both are dynastically-minded people who will unconsciously get one another's scent and instantly decide that the other has what's needed to continue the family line. There's no doubt that there's a big love between them. It's as if they've been looking for one another their whole lives. When they finally meet there's a sense of completion that will be continued on into the next phase of their journey together. Since they are working toward the same goals, they share a feeling of security and joint purpose that make this relationship as easy as riding a tandem bike. The Capricorn man is a serious lover who never leaves his lady guessing as to his devotion. Even when he's at his most practical and purposeful, she'll know that it's because he wants to take the weight off her shoulders and onto his. He'll love the way she fusses over him, so her protective instincts couldn't find a better object. These two will be riding off into the sunset together.

In bed: Procreation is recreation when it comes to the Cancer woman and Capricorn man. They won't be able to leave each other alone until they hear the sound of many tiny pattering feet around their home. Okay, well, they can wait, they but both feel instinctively that this is their objective when they are together. But don't worry. It doesn't end when their kids are grown, for the love between them is everlasting. Now back to the basics. These two have an instinct for getting down and dirty with one another. The Capricorn man can be gentle yet penetrating, so Lady Cancer will soon happily slip out of her protective shell and into something much more comfortable—like his bed! He'll certainly rise to the occasion and satisfy all the Cancer woman's needs, yet he possesses the sensitivity to know when she only wants a cuddle. Her little sideways seduction movements will intrigue and entice him, but he won't miss a trick when it comes to the possibility of being with her in an intensely intimate, magical clinch. They'll keep each other forever limber and lithe for their bedroom antics. He'll go on and on, because the delicate yet exciting sensual responses of his Cancer woman will urge him on to higher levels of passion. She'll completely lose track of time, which will fly when she has her fun, but she may soon decide that early nights are the only answer to her continual lack of sleep.

CANCER WOMAN WITH AQUARIUS MAN

In love: From her viewpoint it appears to Cancer woman that she looks after her Aquarius man in ways he doesn't even know he needs. She's so into mothering that she can be like a surrogate parent at times. But from his point of view, this can amount to smothering. It's not that he doesn't appreciate her efforts, especially at the beginning. However, having been born under an Air sign, he needs to breathe and he likes his independence. He also likes to shake things up a bit, create some mayhem, and cause some shockwaves. Her watery nature is clannish and clinging, which means that she'll be the conductor to his electricity until the result is a raging, angry storm that has them both running for cover. He doesn't show his emotions openly and his aloof and somewhat dogmatic approach to life can really irritate her. She may end up thinking he's simply cold and unfeeling. It's true that he's a cool Water-Bearer but even so, there's a part of him that might just need the Cancer lady's warmth. And there's a big part of her that revels in his colorful mind. He's never short of ideas and that feeds her creative spark. This is a union that could work out as long as they lay all their cards on the table so both can see what they're in for.

In bed: The Aquarius man needs to proceed with caution if he wants to open the Cancer woman's mind to some of the more diverse—she might say kinky—possibilities available to them as sexual partners. She needs to be cuddled and caressed and she doesn't normally like to be completely naked, but if he's patient and able to gain her trust, he could pull it off—along with her clothes. There is a strange fascination between these two and their sexual relationship could be deeply moving for them both. If she's willing to accept that he's not going to give an overt display of emotional commitment, and if he can work at being affectionate while also being sexually stimulating, then they could be surprised at how compulsive their lovemaking could be. Their lovemaking could very well become an extremely titillating pastime. If he would simply relax into the experience of being pampered, then her gentleness and soft caresses could drive him wild with excitement rather than simply excite his irritation. They won't find it easy to understand one another without words but if they can spell out their needs and wants, this will not only be the precursor to some wonderful lovemaking, but will also bring them closer to a divine sexual experience.

CANCER WOMAN WITH PISCES MAN

In love: Put two Water signs together—particularly the Pisces man and the Cancer woman—and what will the result be? A sublime sea of love and emotion. Words can't describe the depth of their mutual affection and understanding; they are almost telepathic in their ability to understand each other's needs and desires. In fact, they'll probably find that if they ever do need to talk, they'll end up doing so in sync. Once they become an item, they'll be finishing each other's sentences then giggling at themselves. To some extent, they'll love each other more as a couple than as individuals. Both are highly sensitive and appreciate the other's qualities equally. She makes him feel like a playful, happy child one minute, then inspires him to want to take care of her and spoil her the next. He can actually be what she wants him to be by being himself! He loves it that she admires his all-encompassing perspective on life and he delights in sharing his view with her. Together they can make a magical, mystical world that only the two of them share—a place where they can let their imaginations flow. But the result won't simply be romantic nonsense that serves no purpose other than to fuel the intoxication of their hearts. They'll probably also be sowing the seeds of a more artistic and successful way of life together. These two inspire one another to achieve more both spiritually and materially than either could achieve on their own.

In bed: The Cancer woman and the Pisces man in bed are what erotic novels are made of. Their lovemaking reaches heights of ecstasy and passion that she never dreamed possible. He'll see only her elemental feminine beauty so she won't need to worry about the odd zit appearing on her face, while she's his ultimate fantasy woman, tender, responsive, and embracing. If she's a little reticent at times and presents a tough, impenetrable wall when he's busy pursuing her, he'll gently change course and find a way to dissolve her defenses until she reveals her soft, sweet center. The Pisces man may sometimes seem to drift off into a world of his own while making love to his lovely Cancer woman, but her imagination is as powerful as his, so there's no reason why she can't drift off with him. All this love, romance, and fantasy may sound wet and wimpish, but this is really more to do with what is going on in their hearts. When it comes to animal passion and erotic pleasure, there will be nothing wimpish about these two. Their relationship is about idealism made real. It just gets better and better as time goes on.

THE CANCER MAN IN LOVE

The Cancer man has everything a woman could want—and then some. He's the epitome of sensitivity and sympathy and is polite, romantic, and an excellent provider. He's also caring, considerate, and probably a good cook, and will protect and look after his woman as though she's a treasured, delicate flower. But it's the "and then some" that might be cause for concern. He's a moody man; one minute he's all hugs and kisses, but the next he's complaining about everyone and about how people just don't realize how much he gives…and so on, and so on. After a few minutes it'll dawn on her that he's actually talking about her, but like the Crab, he goes sideways about it. This can be hurtful, but it's just his defense mechanism and she'll need to get used to it if she intends to spend more than a few nights with him.

The problem is, he's extremely security-conscious, and this manifests itself in a number of ways. Firstly, there's his own security—his self-confidence. The Cancer man needs a lot of reassurance, but to a degree that's almost impossible to provide. He may well set up a few tests and trials in order to find out if his one true love is going to stay with him forever—and long before he brings her home to meet mother.

Next comes the fact that he's very perceptive when it comes to a woman's feelings. He's also a superb lover and knows how to navigate a woman's body without being told, picking up on her subtle moans and gentle shifts in body temperature like some supersonic radar system. With his antenna at full stretch, he'll zero in on his lady's erogenous zones and drive her to complete heavenly ecstasy. And he also has a super-soft shoulder to cry on whenever she needs one. He's great at containing the outpourings of a sad heart and will not only bring the box of tissues, but will be using them, too. Which brings us to the fact that he's also very sensitive about his own feelings, and this is what can make this crabby man downright cantankerous at times.

Still, he can more than make up for this because his feelings about security relate to financial security, too. He's never short of cash and can well afford to buy what a woman needs—yes, that's "needs" rather than "wants." It's not that he's stingy, just that he's savvy when it comes to finances. He knows how to make a buck and save it for a rainy day. So, don't expect to get the biggest, best, grandest, or most expensive of anything. He'll go for quality because it generally lasts longer. And this is the sum of the Cancer man—good quality and great value.

CANCER MAN WITH **ARIES WOMAN**

 In love: The Cancer man will make the most cozy, warm, and inviting home any woman could ever hope for; however, the Aries girl is far too busy to take much notice. That's not to say that all his efforts will be unappreciated; it's just that she's not the most domesticated creature in the world, and if someone else is catering to her needs in that area, then she'll return the favor by providing all sorts of spontaneous fun and excitement. "Well, that's great," says the Cancer man, "but I've just spent all day preparing the perfect romantic dinner, so do we really need to go out partying tonight?" And the Aries girl replies, "But we did the whole romantic dinner thing last week!" That's it: his feelings are hurt, she's totally at a loss to see why, and nobody ends up enjoying themselves, at least not if they spend the evening together. However, if they do have a mutual aim in life, together they can make a very strong team. They both have an ability to dive into the unknown and to give every single ounce of energy to a good cause. As long as the Cancer man doesn't make it his business to try to capture the Aries woman, this coupling could work. If she's ever feeling down, this man will give her the boost she needs; he'll hold her in his protective arms and let her know exactly where she belongs. She'll never want for comfort while she's with him. He's a clannish man and if the Aries girl is into it, she'll soon find she's been adopted into his family.

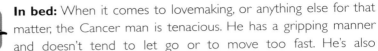 **In bed:** When it comes to lovemaking, or anything else for that matter, the Cancer man is tenacious. He has a gripping manner and doesn't tend to let go or to move too fast. He's also determined to be the instrument of his woman's pleasure so he won't let the Aries woman down in her demand for sexual satisfaction, though some adjustments will be necessary. The Cancer man performs best in the bedroom when there is a heavy emotional content to the proceedings. He doesn't get off on the purely animalistic. He'll do his duty of course, as he's an excellent provider, but it might just lack the passionate fervor that the Aries woman needs if she's going to want a repeat performance. And as she usually likes all-night repeats and re-runs, she had better be able to show him that she's got some depth to her feelings. She won't be able to fake it either, because he's incredibly intuitive and will immediately spot a sham. She will have to get in touch with her inner self at least during the physical part of this relationship. In return, he will reach the deep, dark depths that she would previously not have been aware of. He will make her feel cherished and emotionally secure but he's moody, so, if she still wants to give him a go, she'll need to try to ebb and flow with the Cancer ups and downs.

CANCER MAN WITH **TAURUS WOMAN**

 In love: When the Taurus woman gets together with the Cancer man, romantic Venus meets protective Moon and both planets shine out in the heavenly night skies, radiating a sense of warmth and security. This is exactly what these two lovers do for each other. Their cozy coupling is based on emotional and physical accord. Add that to their mutual love of comfort and luxury, and the result is a glowing combination. They share the same ideals and both have a sixth sense about how to enhance each other's natural ability to bring in the money that will buy their own perfect piece of paradise. Two people who are so much on the same wavelength can't help but be in love. There is a playful friendship between them and acceptance of each other's foibles, so when they get together, problems just seem to fade away. Both are sensitive and emotional. She revels in the romantic; he's receptive and responsive. In many ways they're a reflection of one another, each feeling a deep sense of empathy with the other. He, however, can be changeable and grumpy, needing to protect himself from the constant barrage of emotions that assault him from the outside world. This can destabilize the Lady Bull, who demands constancy and dislikes being emotionally relegated, although with her natural patience and determination to see things through, once he changes back again, it doesn't take long for them to pick up from where they left off. In fact, her stubbornness could easily be the cause of this "crabby" man's retreat into his shell, but it's also one of the qualities he finds most attractive in her since he needs a strong sense of security in order to show off his talents. Once in each other's hearts, they will have a fine romance that they'll find it difficult to get out of.

In bed: This is a mesmerizing experience for them both. They could get so seriously lost in one another that they forget simple little things like the time of day. However, one thing that won't be forgotten is mealtimes. They're both big food-lovers, so their lovemaking may well include some gastronomic specialties to heighten the delicious effect, while her supreme sensuality will never fail to feed the Cancer man's ravenous hunger for her body. The Taurus lady may be a little clumsy at first, as she takes charge of her strong physical desires and attunes them to her Cancer lover, but meanwhile, he'll go with the flow, reaching her most sensitive zones—and she has lots of those. This is a very sexy lady who adores the feeling of physical closeness and gives her body over completely to the experience of making love. Whatever the mood of her Cancer man, she'll succeed in exciting him and he'll make his enjoyment of giving her physical pleasure very obvious, which suits the Taurus woman just fine, because nothing turns her on more. This is the ultimate bedroom encounter, with one player as adoring as the other. She will never fail to fulfill his physical needs and he will fulfill hers as often as she likes.

CANCER MAN WITH GEMINI WOMAN

 In love: The Cancer man could easily fall for the vivacious Gemini girl in a big, big way. He's totally susceptible to her sense of humor and her flirty femininity, and she intrigues and delights him with her childlike innocence. Also, since she has a constantly shifting viewpoint herself, she's a woman who will be totally comfortable with his changeable moods. She won't really understand where he's coming from because his shifts take place at an emotional level, while hers are purely cerebral, but because she can't figure him out, she'll be hooked by him and totally fascinated. He'll probably be able to get a grip on her more easily than she on him, which could make her uncomfortable. A more fickle Gemini girl should go easy on the Cancer man; he's effortlessly enticed into her arms but incredibly sensitive and easily hurt. He longs to forge a deep and intimate familiarity between himself and his partner and desires to create a safe and secure, all-consuming partnership, so unless she's serious, it would be a mistake to mess with him: she may find him harder to lose than a tattoo. This attachment, at least in its early stages, is enough to bring the Gemini girl out in hives; she gets incredibly nervous and even more flighty than usual when her freedom is threatened. The Cancer man, for all his commitment, won't remain enamored for long if she doesn't show at least some emotional depth. He'll scuttle away sideways and never be seen again.

 In bed: The Cancer man may look tough, but underneath that hard shell he's as soft as butter. He wants to spend long romantic evenings walking along the seashore and talking his Gemini girl into bed, which is wonderful and really works for her. However, the moment will come during that long walk when her imagination will have been captured, and she'll be ready to cut to the chase. Droning on in that lovey-dovey voice of his will only spoil her excitement. She's running out of patience. She wants him now! If she touches him gently he'll melt into her arms then hold her firmly in his claws. The sexual temperature could rise to boiling point! Her selection of sex toys may frighten the fragile Crab a little, at least until he feels that the relationship is steady and that they're in bed together for the long haul. He's a natural man and doesn't feel the need for any enhancement in order to get her high, or vice versa, but he's accommodating to the needs and wishes of his irresistible Gemini girl. Although these two are essentially different, they're also deliciously compatible because they have so much to discover. All in all, there's plenty of thrilling anticipation.

CANCER MAN WiTH **CANCER WOMAN**

See pages 59–60.

CANCER MAN WiTH **LEO WOMAN**

 In love: At times these two will really enjoy being together and will generate plenty of warmth, comfort, and mutual goodwill, with a great sense of shared well-being. The openly loving Cancer man will touch the Leo lady's heart most sincerely and, on one of his good days, he knows exactly how to make her feel like a queen. But if she comes face to face with him on one of his moody days, she'll be perplexed at what to do with all his swamping emotion. If it's one of her good days, she'll handle him in her naturally merciful and noble manner, but push her too far on a bad day, and she's likely to take a swipe at him. Then he'll have to wake up and smell the coffee! But there's no real need for them to worry. He gets out of his doldrums really fast and she'll soon be back in top form and full of sweet, caring, embracing love. She's very generous when it comes to gifts and she can be sure that the Cancer man will treasure everything she gives him. However, she'll be a little perplexed and peeved if all his gifts to her are of the domestic kind. She wants Versace, not vacuum cleaners! If he's one of the less moody, more gregarious Crabs, then there's a lot to recommend this relationship, but if not, it might be best if she lets him scuttle away. Then this lioness can go back to roaming the savanna once more.

 In bed: The tender, gentle, intuitive lovemaking that the Cancer man is expert at is the perfect tonic for this luxury-loving Leo lady, particularly when she's in one of her languorous, lounging moods. The trouble is that she's unlikely to stay in it once her libido has been livened up and he'll know when he's turned her on because she'll very quickly become a wild cat—perhaps a bit too much of one for the gentle Cancer man. She'll want something to sink her teeth into, so he'll probably end up with a few more nibble marks or scratches on his back than he had planned. The Lady Lion instinctively leaps into action whenever he strokes her mane or ruffles her fur. He's very instinctive and can play the hard man when the occasion calls for it, but he mostly prefers to take a softer, more emotional approach to erotic intimacy. Her animal appetites need a rapturous response, but since his rapture shows itself as calm, careful sweetness, she simply won't understand it. He has claws too, but his merely hold onto her and never let go. He may pour all his heartfelt loving tenderness over her but he could end up drowning her raging fire. It's definitely a matter of timing.

CANCER MAN WITH VIRGO WOMAN

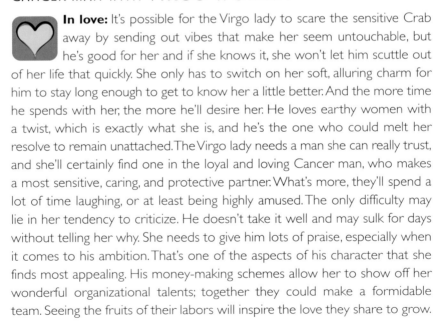

In love: It's possible for the Virgo lady to scare the sensitive Crab away by sending out vibes that make her seem untouchable, but he's good for her and if she knows it, she won't let him scuttle out of her life that quickly. She only has to switch on her soft, alluring charm for him to stay long enough to get to know her a little better. And the more time he spends with her, the more he'll desire her. He loves earthy women with a twist, which is exactly what she is, and he's the one who could melt her resolve to remain unattached. The Virgo lady needs a man she can really trust, and she'll certainly find one in the loyal and loving Cancer man, who makes a most sensitive, caring, and protective partner. What's more, they'll spend a lot of time laughing, or at least being highly amused. The only difficulty may lie in her tendency to criticize. He doesn't take it well and may sulk for days without telling her why. She needs to give him lots of praise, especially when it comes to his ambition. That's one of the aspects of his character that she finds most appealing. His money-making schemes allow her to show off her wonderful organizational talents; together they could make a formidable team. Seeing the fruits of their labors will inspire the love they share to grow.

In bed: Both these individuals are very caring with those they love, and as long as they can keep this caring on the physical, as well as the emotional level, their love will stay alive forever. These two have a fresh, friendly approach to intimacy and they naturally accept and understand the unspoken side of the other's erotic desires. When she gets into a lovemaking frame of mind, the Virgo lady has a delightfully skillful touch. She loves to look after his bodily needs just as much as he likes to caress her emotionally and physically. He'll know how to open up her feelings for him by pushing all the right buttons and she'll instinctively make that earthy physical connection with him. Her demure, butter-wouldn't-melt-in-the-mouth exterior will come tumbling down to expose a fierce sexuality. Their lovemaking is perfectly matched; however, both can be shy at first, so their relationship needs time to develop. Give them years together and their lovemaking will mature into something very beautiful, long after most people are well past their expiration date.

CANCER MAN WITH LIBRA WOMAN

 In love: Cancer man's gentleness and sensitivity make it easy for the Libra lady to love him. She is naturally drawn to his refined manner and he is immediately intrigued by her delicate beauty. Both enjoy surrounding themselves with beautiful things, so homemaking will be a shared pleasure. At first glance, it looks as if Mr. Crab is the man the Libra lady has been looking for, and together they can make a real love nest.

If she's ever feeling blue, he'll wrap his arms snugly around her, but he's also happy to go along for the ride when her spirits are high. That is, unless he's in one of his dark moods and she's in one of her flirty phases—perhaps flirting with one of his friends. He won't just sit there and take it. He'll be vocal in his displeasure until she may feel as though she's drowning in a sea of his emotions. At these times they simply won't connect. He'll be demanding reassurance and wanting to be mothered, just when she's in the mood to go out and party! Their relationship can sometimes be downright difficult, sometimes deliriously delightful. In other words, it won't always be harmonious but it won't be hellish either. Such is the changeable nature of Libra and the moodiness of Cancer when they're together. At best, they'll have a beautifully dynamic partnership. At worst, it could become a competition to see who's better at making the other one feel guilty. Unless they're both winners, both will lose out.

 In bed: The sexual side of the Cancer man and Libra woman relationship begins long before these two get between the sheets. It starts when she flutters her eyelashes at him and he "accidentally" brushes his hand across her breast. They'll titillate and tease one another into a heightened state of desire to make sure that the other is fully committed before getting undressed. Once they're actually in bed, the sexual experience for the Cancer man and Libra lady involves a lot of ups and downs. Get ready to get emotional. This man can make such beautiful love that she could end up crying with the sweetness of it. And he's not afraid of her tears; in fact, he'll adore her even more for her display of emotion. However, there could sometimes be a conflict between her need for light and easy lovemaking and his for a deeper connection. It's a roller-coaster ride that's both scary and fun. It will be a moving experience, one way or another, and he won't be quick to let go when she wants to get off, which means that the next round of tears could be caused by something altogether different.

CANCER MAN WITH SCORPIO WOMAN

 In love: A love supreme! There's obviously a very natural flow of energy between these two when they first meet and whenever they get together thereafter. The Cancer man will win the Scorpio lady over completely with his gentle, loving ways and will totally adore her. She knows it, and although the Scorpio lady finds it very difficult to entrust her heart to someone, she'll finally have met the soul with whom it's possible. He'll never tread on her feelings and will care for her and protect her from anything that could possibly trouble her. She'll be happy to accept him together with all the depth of feeling he possesses, which he hides from the rest of the world. However, her need to really get to the bottom of him will, because of his constantly shifting emotions, be a labor of love that could last her a lifetime. He sees her love as a precious gift and will treat it that way, and although his moods can go up and down like a yo-yo and can become a little irritating, her unwavering strength will see her through. However, her tendency to lash out when she's feeling vulnerable could hurt him more than she'll ever know. That's the worst-case scenario, but all in all, there's so much harmony in this relationship that the very few, minor irritations in it can easily be overcome. These two simply intoxicate each other with their compulsive, addictive love. This is one very happy union.

 In bed: This man's the Scorpio lady's perfect prey. She won't just see him coming, she'll feel his vibe from way off, almost as though she's expecting him. But while she uses her special arts of seduction, his tough outer shell will give nothing away. He'll probably just sit there motionless, like a Crab, even though he's churning with lascivious desire. He wants her badly but somehow knows that if he gives in too soon, she'll lose interest. She likes a challenge, and he's happy to present her with one, then, just as her desire to have him reaches fever pitch, he'll surrender with a sweet eroticism and make love to her until she's left completely breathless. These two know exactly how to get to one another's sexual core. The Scorpio lady's intense sexual passion is palpable but it's so deeply rooted in her emotional connection with her partner that it takes an equally emotionally tuned-in lover to satisfy her. Unless they're those rare demonstrative types who can't keep their hands off each other, the subtlety they display in front of other people completely belies what's really going on between these two. They share a deep yet very playful eroticism and they're so sweet with each other. This pair are made for each other—they fit together like spoons.

CANCER MAN WITH **SAGITTARIUS WOMAN**

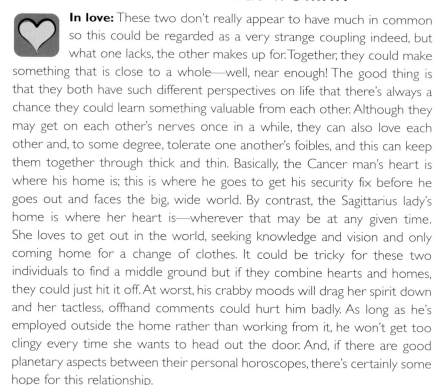

In love: These two don't really appear to have much in common so this could be regarded as a very strange coupling indeed, but what one lacks, the other makes up for. Together, they could make something that is close to a whole—well, near enough! The good thing is that they both have such different perspectives on life that there's always a chance they could learn something valuable from each other. Although they may get on each other's nerves once in a while, they can also love each other and, to some degree, tolerate one another's foibles, and this can keep them together through thick and thin. Basically, the Cancer man's heart is where his home is; this is where he goes to get his security fix before he goes out and faces the big, wide world. By contrast, the Sagittarius lady's home is where her heart is—wherever that may be at any given time. She loves to get out in the world, seeking knowledge and vision and only coming home for a change of clothes. It could be tricky for these two individuals to find a middle ground but if they combine hearts and homes, they could just hit it off. At worst, his crabby moods will drag her spirit down and her tactless, offhand comments could hurt him badly. As long as he's employed outside the home rather than working from it, he won't get too clingy every time she wants to head out the door. And, if there are good planetary aspects between their personal horoscopes, there's certainly some hope for this relationship.

In bed: Initially, the physical attraction between these two could be very strong and very sexy. The Sagittarius lady will sense Mr. Cancer's brooding sexuality and she is always prepared to try anything once. He may find a few steamy nights of hot and heavy sex rather sweet, but unless she can offer him at least a token of her commitment, the Cancer man might simply back away from her into his protective shell. She's a wild one and he'd love to be with her, but he won't be sure of himself when he's around her. He'll always wonder whether or not he measures up to her more adventurous style. Sure, he can try to tie her down, but she won't like it because she's into having fun in the bedroom and any restrictions will simply put her fire out. For his part, the Cancer man is very emotional and he needs to feel secure with his sexual partner or else he gets crabby and moody. Will the Sagittarius woman be able to react appropriately? She's very sexually, if not emotionally, tuned-in, so at least her lusty passionate side will give him a modicum of contentment, but he could begin to feel a little like a sex-object after a while. Most men would probably revel in this, but if the Cancer man feels that he's only being appreciated for his ability to play the bedroom love-toy, he'll eventually get quite depressed. An agreement to have an on-off relationship would keep the heat on high with this couple, but that may just be a bridge too far for the commitment-seeking Cancer man.

CANCER MAN WITH CAPRICORN WOMAN

 In love: In many ways, the Capricorn woman and Cancer man were made for each other. They have an instinct about each other and they understand each other totally, even before they've had a chance to have a heart to heart. The attraction between them is enormous and they have such similar intentions that they can get lost in each other completely, forgetting who said what or did what. The gentle, caring Cancer man makes the Capricorn lady go weak at the knees, and she has such a very special talent for building up his self-esteem that she makes him feel good about himself as no one else can. And why wouldn't she? He has that deep-rooted sensitivity and action-oriented quality that she so admires. When these two get together it feels as though the world has set itself to rights. They make a truly formidable team as they're both ambitious and they both feel happier when there's someone to share the fruits of their labor with. Many a night will pass with the two of them curled up on a comfortable sofa together, drinking fine wine from the family crystal, and congratulating each other on their successes. But there is a downside: the Cancer man has a tendency toward frequent moodiness and if one of his dark moods coincides with one of hers, then it could all feel a little heavy around their place. Most of the time however, their realistic, stable, and heartwarming love just grows and grows.

In bed: These two are not so shy around one another as they can be with other Sun signs. When they're together they have the feeling that they can be totally themselves and they are uninhibited. Her passion is all tightly coiled intensity, while his is languorous and relaxed, so he'll push this way and she'll pull that way. Although it might seem as if they're coming at it from different perspectives, somehow it always works out in the end and satisfaction's guaranteed. It goes like this with these two: he's a real nester. He wants to provide the perfect, comfortable space in which she can uncurl all her erotic energy in his direction. If he has a day off work, he could spend it all in bed with her by his side and she won't mind, since being physically close to her lover is what life, for her, is all about. And although she'll want to have her fair share of taking the initiative, she's quite happy to cozy up under his warm blanket and be held with the tightness that the Cancer man is famous for. If she wants to try something a little different, it won't rumble him. She could start by making a picnic on the bed since, as far as he's concerned, food and sex go together like sand and sea. He'll be glad to help pack the basket with lots of tasty things, and then he'll provide the dessert for his delicious Capricorn lady.

CANCER MAN WITH AQUARIUS WOMAN

 In love: The attraction between these two lies in the fact that both are fascinated by the strange, abstract, and mystical side of life and both find the other strange, abstract, and mystical, too!

The sweet Cancer man will pull hard at the alluring Aquarius lady's heartstrings, which will not be a comfortable experience for her. She prefers discretion and friendship, and though she likes to talk, she prefers, if at all possible, not to talk about personal feelings. He'll find her aloof sophistication an irresistible challenge and will do his utmost to extract an emotional response from her. If none is forthcoming he'll feel crushed and then he'll tell her that it's all her fault! She won't be able to see why she should take the blame when she's done nothing wrong…and so it goes on. The Cancer man is all about emotional attachment, while she prefers emotional detachment. She may find him deliciously interesting and extremely attractive, but keeping him happy could be too much like hard work. One thing that fills her with fear is his possessiveness and his need for nurturing; the Aquarius girl isn't against commitment, it's simply that she's too involved with humanity as a whole to focus all her care and attention on just one person. It won't be easy for them to find a middle ground, but never say never. Even if it doesn't happen in this space–time continuum, there's always a chance that these two will find their way together to heaven and beyond!

In bed: The Aquarius girl has an unconventional approach to sex so she won't get off on romance and tenderness. The first time she hears those sweet violins while the romantic Cancer man is kissing and caressing her, she'll no doubt feel shivers all over. But by the second, let alone the twentieth time, her eyes will probably wander to the clock and she'll be wondering what time her friends are meeting up. He wants to feel loved and nurtured, and needs to develop a deep emotional bond in order to get his sexuality pumping, while she likes a bit of unpredictability and some shock tactics. She'd really love her Cancer man to be spontaneous, show up when she's out meeting up with her pals, and pounce on her. He, of course, would feel totally adored if she blew going out with her friends and instead stayed home and let her gentle airy breeze blow over him. These two just don't get where the other's coming from. He would take it as a personal insult to his prowess if she ever suggested something a little kinky, even just rock music instead of the violins.

CANCER MAN WITH **PISCES WOMAN**

 In love: This is a beautiful, precious, perfect love. Emotionally, the Pisces lady and the Cancer man give and receive in equal proportions, spiritually, physically, and mentally. Things could hardly be better and since both are Water signs, they meld and flow into one another. When the world feels a little threatening and all she wants is someone to hold her, he'll be there, and when he needs to forget about his troubles, she can take him out of himself with her love. The only problem is that they could get so caught up in their own private world that things of a more practical nature are ignored. But the Cancer man will be there to gently bring them back to reality and, strangely, he's never so crabby when he's around her. If he does get into a mood, she'll be able to look beyond it and carry on as usual, knowing that it will pass as surely as the tides will change.

In fact, she's so inclined to drift off into her own dreamy realms, she may not even have noticed his bad mood in the first place and this, most of the time, is what her Cancer man would prefer. While these two are floating away on their fluffy pink clouds to the sound of angels singing, they'll need to spare a thought for the mere mortals of the world. Once they've found each other, they'll never want to let go. This is as close to perfect as it can get.

In bed: This is transcendental sex, the most uplifting sort of sensuality! These two find themselves having an out-of-body experience every time their very real bodies are writhing together on the bed. They've found their perfect partner in passion and it's enough to make them weep for joy. Is this an exaggeration? Not at all! If they go out to friends for dinner, they'll either make their excuses and leave early so they can be alone, or else they'll sneak off to the bathroom at the same time. When they eventually float back to the dining table, the look on their faces will confirm to everyone exactly what they've been up to—and they won't even be embarrassed! They're always blissfully unaware of anyone else when the other is in the room. The spirit of this relationship is intoxicating and the physical side is heart-stopping. Yes, he does like to have deep roots planted in the ground and she likes to flow free, but this difference works to their advantage. She won't let him get away with his usual conventionality, and he'll love it, and he simply won't let her get away.